TRAVELER

TRAVELER

DEVIN JOHNSTON

FARRAR, STRAUS AND GIROUX

NEW YORK

FARRAR, STRAUS AND GIROUX

18 West 18th Street, New York 10011

Copyright © 2011 by Devin Johnston

Distributed in Canada by D&M Publishers, Inc.

Printed in the United States of America

First edition, 2011

Library of Congress Cataloging-in-Publication Data

Johnston, Devin.

Traveler / Devin Johnston.— 1st ed.

p. cm.

ISBN 978-0-374-27933-2 (cloth : alk. paper)

I. Title.

PS3610.O385 T73 2011

811'.6—dc22

2011008457

Designed and composed by Quemadura

www.fsgbooks.com

1 3 5 7 9 10 8 6 4 2

CONTENTS

The lines of this new song are nothing
But a tune making the nothing full . . .

LOUIS ZUKOFSKY

TRAVELER

FROM MEDICINE LODGE

From Medicine Lodge
to Coldwater, from Coldwater
to Protection and beyond,
this undulating line
intersects no industry
yet slows to Central,
resumes a bare number,
and finally frays
in shallow tracks
where Black Kettle
and Standing Feather
took their geologic time
and left no cairn.

Salt and gypsum collapsed
to form a basin
shadows race across,
their smooth momentum
broken only
by a spindly windmill

with its corrugated trough
or scratchy, windrattled
cottonwood, a graph
of fluctuating force,
anything upright
under revision.

A twist of hair
threads the ring
of a dried-up sink
as stackenclouds and fibrous
sonderclouds draw silver
from common sagebrush,
or waneclouds streak
the afternoon with grains
of polished wood—
only to kindle flame
as everything shuts down
but cloudworks, unfinished
parts of a world.

NOTHING SONG

after William IX, Duke of Aquitaine

I made this up from nothing.
It's not myself I sing,
or love, or anything
    that has a source.
I dreamed these words while riding
    on my horse.

I've neither youth nor age.
Ambitions out of range,
I feel no joy or rage
    to see them go.
One midnight worked the change
    that made me so.

I wonder, do I wake
from dreams, or dream I wake?
Beneath a sheet, I shake
    and clutch my heart,
though part of me—aloof, opaque—
    remains apart.

For such uncertainty
I've found no remedy
in psychotherapy
    or sedatives.
I rummage through debris
    where nothing lives.

A friend I've never met,
unknown to me as yet,
has kindled no regret
    or happiness,
no tender sobriquet
    to curse or bless.

As coldly radiant
as stars, and light-years distant,
this expectation can't
    embrace a life,
but shines on, ignorant
    of lust and strife.

My song of nothing done,
I ride from Avignon
and leave my words to one
    who turns a key
to find the deadbolt drawn
    and stable empty.

EXPECTING

what will she
now a she

trailing clouds
yet hearing our

muffled voices
all the while

from this dark
world and wide

what will she
mew or bray

as any envoy
might derive

an embryon
from animal

or amnion
from tender lamb

though tethered to
a human form

an embryon
in amnion

or bloom of jellies
at the whim

of storm and tide
the ocean's roar

above, around,
and then inside

AUBADE

A vacant hour
before the sun—
and with it a valve's
pneumatic hush,
the deep and nautical
clunk of wood,
chanson du ricochet
of rivet gun,
trowel tap,
and bolt drawn—

the moon sets
and water breaks.

Curled within
a warm pleroma,
playing for time,
you finally turn
and push your face

toward November's
glint of frost,
grains of salt,
weak clarities
of dawn.

CESAREAN

Graphing pain,
the toco monitor
scrolls a white
bounding line
on a blue field:
not heraldry but
a lightning flash
illuminates
the rugged range
of your estate,
from deep crevasse
to trackless slopes
of Traversette.
Dryly tapping,
a clerical ghost
prints a pan-
oramic strip.
In a sudden charge,
the air contracts
a vast expanse

(remote and thin)
to this bare room
where surgeons cut
a Gordian knot
and everyone
says *wonderful*
when they forget.

TRAVELER

From the foot of Cotopaxi
and across the Gulf

a Blackburnian warbler
follows a pulse,

follows Polaris
and the Pole's magnetic field

through travail
and travel's long ordeal,

until he drops
to a black walnut's
pinnate leaves

tossing like waves
in the North Sea

and glances toward
my lamplit, stationary world
of smooth planes:

against a cloud,
his throat's flame.

FOREIGN OBJECT

The hours spent on transpacific flights
pass like a sandstorm through the Mongol steppes,
lodging a single grain—an irritant
to memory—within the furrowed cortex.
Nacred by revolving doubt, it grows
a pearl as black as the ocean depths
and lustrous as the moon
through sublimated ice.

This pearl outlives its host—and can be bought
in Shanghai, from an unassuming shop
on the French Concession's western edge.
The jeweler plucks it from a velvet box
and cups the pearl like a Dramamine
in the hollow of her outstretched palm.
She stands like that, expectantly,
revolving shapes to come.

ROGET'S THESAURUS

At the first surge of psychotic trance,
to ward it off or ride it out,
Peter Roget took up a list:
breeds of dogs, human bones, anatomies
of cloud, or forms of transport.
It steadied his mind to study the spokes
of wheels glimpsed through vertical slats:
van, wagon, whisky, tumbrel, truck;
the blur of whips and hooves,
ornate signage stripped of syntax.

Now, among aseptic cells
of Bonne Terre, Roget's thesaurus
circulates more than Malcolm X.
One offender, stout as a mule,
circles the yard while leafing through
a dog-eared passage (cf. *trough*)
from *hole* to *eye* to *aperture* and on:
outlet, inlet, orifice, throat,

channel, chimney, pit, pore,
sieve, riddle, borer, screw,
bodkin, needle, warder, gouge.

As an officer calls for head count,
the morning sun reticulates
filigree of chain link
and a curl of concertina wire.
It glances off the hubcap
of a distant Cadillac
joining the flow of traffic.

NOWHERE

Sifu John has left the dojo
and struck out on his own.
No more shit from Master Jong,
no endless adjudications
of single whip, no banquets,
belts, dues, or membership.

His only student—big dude
with the tight, slick ponytail
of Steven Seagal—
got lit and locked
a bartender in tiger claw,
then spent a night in jail.

Clearly distinguish
empty from full,
the classics instruct.

Mornings, feeling thick, John
crosses off his mother's list

at Schnucks, returning home
with tourniquets of plastic bags.

Evenings, sifu and student
grasp the sparrow's tail
beside a picnic pavilion
perched above the park's basin,
its pooling shadows
emptied of pedestrians.

As snow begins to fall,
they return to fundamentals
of *Peng, Lu, Ji, An* . . .
slow as three-toed sloths
under the orange glare
of sodium lights
with all else thrown in darkness.
Getting nowhere.

SET APART

Set apart
from the compound
friction of forest,
a rough-barked
bur oak,
mostly trunk,
outlives
its understory.

A sapling in 1700,
it rose like smoke
from leaf litter,
a totem for those
who told tales
vertically,
every episode
the offspring
of earth and sky.

Carotenoids flare
through its vascular system
in slow time,
releasing aromas
of black tea
and tobacco.

Winter-hardened,
the oak endures,
a column supporting
nothing but its own
fixed extension.

The fine point
of a feeding warbler—
a drifting spark
or cursor—
ghosts its crown.

COLD-BLOODED

Beyond a ring
of mercury light
nothing conspicuous
could survive
the coming night.
The rippling hunch
of a barred owl
propounds as yet
no prey, no rattle
in late September's
coil of fern.
A cold breath
of Brush Creek
gently rocks
joe-pye weed,
but skin still
radiates heat
from the setting sun.
Fever kindles
a turbulent flow

continuous with sleep,
shape-shifting
until an earthen
effigy uncurls
its cursive form
across the ridge.
The snake god
swallows an egg
as Draco slips
through tattered leaves.
Beyond the creek,
a white truck
catches the last
light of day
and sends it back.

HIGH AND LOW

Placid Pan
snores in the sun
as a thunderhead
comes to rest
on the canyon's rim.
From a hump
of high withers
a ridge descends
to a moist rhinarium
or the puckered phrase
e pluribus unum.

Bison bison,
periodic
       as prairie fire,
graze its aftermath
of new grass,
their burnt heads
slung low
and panicked by any

cracked report.
The lightning bolt,
lord of everything,
drawn on a skull
in red ochre,
draws a herd
whose delicate hooves
thunder to raise
a cloud of dust.

STORM AND STURGEON

When a thunderstorm
  trundles down the Wabash,
revealing the form
  of flow in every flash,
northerlies lash
  the walls that keep us warm,
rummaging grass,
  scattering flock and swarm.

Beneath an icy
  column thick as phlegm,
this cold coyote
  of our river system
peers through a scrim
  of silt and leaf debris
as lightning skims
  the shoals of Harmonie.

As each percussion
    shakes the sturgeon's bladder—
a loose vibration
    felt in fleshy matter—
her switch-tail stirs
    beds of hibernation,
bottom dwellers
    lost in cloud formations.

TANGLED YARN

Darner, sewing needle,
exclamation damsel,

pennant, flying adder,
tang- or sanging eater,

fleeing eather, bluet,
steelyard, spindle, booklet,

skimmer, scarce or common,
sand or shadow dragon,

cruiser, shadow damsel,
devil's horse or saddle,

darning needle, dancer,
meadow hawk or glider,

water naiad, threadtail,
sylph or sprite or penny nail.

THE INLAND ROAD

Wake up, wake up,
a kettle yawns
and coughs,
slurring its copper bell
with faint
horns.
Haru-ichiban
with winter gone
clicks
a sharp stick
on walls of stone
and shuffles off
a slough
of plastic sheets.
Somewhere below, a horse
stamps at his trough
and rattles empty stirrups.

EARLY APRIL

Under the Sinclair's brontosaurus sign,
three men collect around a coffeepot
on metal folding chairs. One talks
of rust on a spring-tooth harrow, matters
of cultivation, while the others
ruminate on plastic mugs. Down Route M,
the lek returns to a low ridge
of soy and hissing fescue, booming grounds
abandoned to the long nose of a tractor
where only roans had cast a shadow.

Tympanuchus cupido taught Lakotas
how to dance, its throat patch yellow
as egg yolks, its booming glug
of a low tone swallowed, head feathers erect
in practiced threat. Desire's kettledrum.
Theirs is a culture more intractable
than forbs or Scottish fiddle tunes.

A county south, at Adam-ondi-Ahman,
Mormons wait in a canvas blind
as fog lifts from combed furrows
for a Clovis Christ to come. If he does,
they'll send him up a tree to scout
what's rushing across the low ridge,
whether prairie chicken or machine.
Both live forever until they die.

MARCO POLO

As dusk turns to dark, swallows turn to bats:
their smooth parabolas of flight erode
to flutters. Emitting dry clicks above
the peak of what we hear, they probe
for moth wings. Perched in her high chair,
my daughter echoes the names of things
in early Mandarin or Cantonese.
Each syllable returns—without its edge
of consonants—to test the contours of
a human face. As blue turns to black,
the neighbors' children shout *Marco! Polo!*
in antiphony across the swimming pool,
the sightless id calling to its ego,
groping toward a mark beyond the pale.

Riding through the Gashun Gobi desert
in search of Kublai Khan, a traveler might
nod off and veer from his companions, hearing
voices or the clatter of caravans
through the dark, across the scalloped dunes,

as particles collide in booming sands.
If he follows, dreaming, woe betide him.
So the Mongols fasten little bells
around the necks of camels, goats, and mules.
Their ringing rides along with us like stars.

AT SEA RANCH

Like cordage from a lost rig,
a loose braid of bullwhips
breaches a wave, holdfast
anchors adrift, canopy ripped.
Bladder wrack or black tang
wraps a hollow bulb,
and from each terminal, a stipe
curls in Arabic script.

Darkness can't descend
but rises off the sand,
rising up like fine smoke.
As the tide flows in,
living bullwhips drown
and leave the wrack afloat.

ORACLE BONES

In subdivisions of the dead
a Plum Blossom cigarette
stuck upright
in fresh dirt
glows in a gust of wind.

Counterfeit passports,
subway tickets,
spirit transfers
to offshore accounts,
official chops
for disappearing ink,
paper currency
bearing the watermark
Bank of Heaven, Ltd.,
all burn
for otherworldly use.

Pulling weeds
at the edge of darkness,

trustees undertake
burdens of ownership
as Shang diviners
busy themselves
with hairline cracks
in oracle bones,
ox scapulae
and turtle shells,
filing reports
and currying favor.

Umbrellas open
around an excavation
and all of this world
pours into the next.

THIN PLACE

White ash,
you wait for me

as I will wait
for someone.

What but skin
feels the wind,

what darkness
makes distinctions?

Breaking down
dusk and dawn,

housewreckers
on horse scaffolds

syncopate
their hammers.

Brick dust
drifts like smoke,

tents of habitation
withdrawn,

hinges of habit
undone.

RELATIVES

no one left
the same to say

what it is
that changed

APPETITES

1

My daughter, three, lies awake
talking in confidential tones
with one she calls
my friend who eats me.
Its very name raises the question
of where to draw a line
in affinities and affections.
Like a brook, her voice
burbles down the hall,
on and on, a lilt
of barely suppressed delight.

2

Mrs. Rondinella drifts
six feet above her shadow
in a buoyant chaise longue,
eyes shut in quiet bliss,
fingers interlaced
below her navel.
*She has a baby growing
in her belly*, I explain.
Squinting at the sun,
you speculate,
She swallowed it!

3

Ravenous for each other,
a teenage couple intertwine
in a darkened carport,
eyes shut in concentration,
tongue exploring tongue,
tooth scraping tooth,
on and on, each attuned
to the faint taste
of aluminum;
appetites unslaked.

KID

Before I've shed my scarf and coat,
she's on me, shouting *Kid! We're late!*
Like surf, she batters around my knees,
aggressive joy, insistent need.

Her greeting, mock-tyrannical,
initiates a game or spell,
though one as lightly taken up
as any blossom she begs to clip
and later begs to cast aside.
Hey kid! she crows, and I accede
to misrule—*kid* assumes a force
by which familiar roles reverse.
Outside, a mockingbird explodes
in hectic song, its vocal raids
on chickadee and chimney swift.
We hurry past to catch a flight
to some fantastic Bangladesh,
our destination crudely sketched
in chalk, a scratchy pictograph

of crocodile or banyan leaf.
Invention lags, the day turns cold,
and we resume accustomed roles.

At dusk, while her authority
gives way to sleep, I watch TV:
A Buddhist lama passed away
and left his pupil, Tenzin-Ja,
to scour the land for his rebirth.
The lama's silk hat pointed north
and a giant, star-shaped fungus bloomed
beside the northern wall of his tomb.
Such omens guided Tenzin-Ja
to where a scraggy hamlet lay
like scree beneath its granite slope.
An old man drove a herd of goats
through the gate on which his child
swung at play, the arcing ride
from help to hindrance back to help.
Presented with a row of bells,
the boy, as if awakening
from deep in a trance, grasped and rang
the lama's own. *It's mine, it's mine!*

—a glint of something in his eye
that set his family ill at ease.
So Tenzin-Ja took custody
of the rinpoche who once raised him,
exchanges signaled by a chime.

ROUGH PATCH

You can tell, by symptoms of neglect,
something of his circumstance:
the chipped and buckled eaves, deflated
jack-o'-lantern beside the stoop,
an ember under snow,
or red ants swarming the sill,
crossing a line of cinnamon
in some far-flung military action.
You can tell, by frying onions,
their thick domestic weather,
or the grim satisfaction with which
his vacuum overlooks
a plain of fur and dust.
I can tell from a little
just what a whole lot means.
You treat me like somebody
you ain't never seen.

Hackle stacker, mayfly cripple,
and Bloom's parachute ant

crowd an ashtray—to rarify
the quality of failure.

Mornings, a frowzy Manx
kneads his chest with claws unsheathed,
thrumming with desire
and contempt in equal measure.
Every other weekend, he rolls out
a court-appointed cot
from the closet for his daughter.
You can feel, with your fingertips
against his metal door,
vibrations from the interstate
or seismic evidence
of Furry Lewis,
circa 1928.

CRUMBS

1

You could caulk every crack
and mice would still find ways
through our foundation, sleep
would still get broken,
and we would still
be sweeping up the floor.

2

A hen pecks
the kitchen step
for scratch,

fluffs against
the damp chill,

and scrapes her beak
like a struck match
along the sill.

3

Out of the frozen bed,
a curl of carrot leaf.

Out of sleep, a hand
slides between the sheets.

STATIC

Zipping your skirt, you rustle past,
sand hissing through a glass,
with the bedouin snap and flash
of static-electric
sparks disturbing fabric.
This morning's charge could rouse
The Desert Fathers of Sinai
over which I drowse.

A LOST NOTEBOOK

after Propertius

So my little notebook is gone,
and with it a thousand things I'd written!
Smears from the heel of my hand
authenticate the source, unsigned.
It knew how to please a girl in my absence,
and how, when I would stray,
to turn a soothing phrase.
No split calfskin made it precious:
we're talking college-ruled and spiral-bound.
Whatever the bond, it always procured
the right effect, and always kept its word.

Left on the dining-room table, my notebook
often accreted this sort of thing:
I'm angry you showed up late yesterday.
Did you find someone more lovely?
Or do you intend to fling
a trumped-up charge in my face?
Or else, her looping hand announced,

You'll come today, we'll skip our classes
and mingle on my bed for hours,
and whatever else a keen girl
invents to win an assignation.

What misery! Some frugal bastard
keeps accounts on its blank pages
and shelves it with *The Millionaire Next Door.*
I'll offer a bounty for safe return:
Who'd cling to pulp in lieu of cash?
Hurry, kid, go staple this
to a telephone pole, and indicate
that the owner lives on Sidney Street.

THE YOUNG PRETENDER

Though living in a foreign land,
I recognize my avatars
in every song the washers sing:
the cuckoo is a bonny bird;
my moorhen has feathers enew;
there was a man came from the moon.
But none could recognize a king
who buys his butter on the street
and brings it home in a lettuce leaf.
All the while, I have in mind
a clachan where we passed the night:
sleet against a cottage roof,
a flight of warblers on the pipes,
and dawn before I thought upon
the road, skirting mountains black
beneath a cloud, but silver-laced
with forces where the sun broke through.
By simple reckoning—though math
is not my strength—at twenty-five
I set my foot against the main

with seven true companions
and seized through sheer exuberance
what twenty French battalions
never could. My standard raised
a skirling clan from every bit
and cities fell without a shot.
For seven months I saw through steel
and made it melt, a brain of fire
with feet of ice. Then Culloden:
my skin still prickles at the name.
I sat astride a gray gelding—
a net of lemons slung across
my saddlebow—and stuck a sprig
of Highland heather in my cap
beside the Stuarts' white cockade.
I heard my own high, lisping voice
shout, as from a long way off,
Go on my lads! The day is ours.
What a fool—the heights of young
ambition come to broken eggs.

BURREN

The wisp I once pursued
would utter, drunk or high,
an accusatory *you*
or proud, emphatic *I*,
returning quietly
at break of day to bed
and the old, familiar *we*
she carries in her head:
a village on the crest
of Turlough Hill, a ring
of huts now dispossessed
of any moving thing.
A toppled cairn has wrung
another paradox
of blood from stone and hart's tongue
from grikes in pavement blocks.
Amid dry-stone dikes
of endless iteration—
meanders, copes, and heights
of tireless variation—

a Holstein turns her gaze
from human artifacts
to contemplate the maze
of her digestive tract.
Across the karst from Black Head
and south to Mullach Mór,
sedimental slabs embed
a teeming ocean floor.
Stone from blood: a bluff
arisen from the sea
compressed its lacy cuff
in fossil memory.

IONA

Arriving damp with sea spray, fingers cold,
I disembark a day already old
as billows scatter seeds or smithy sparks
across the west, against the growing dark
of Dalriada, Pictland, Gododdin,
and Strathclyde, shadows flooding every glen.

Birds take flight from nested hierarchies
of class, order, family, genus, species,
in and out of weeks, across an ocean,
skimming foamy paragraphs of Ossian,
an immram of uncertain end or goal
until the island rises from a shoal.

Columbidae *Columba livia*
sails on outstretched wings from its armada,
catching sudden flame above the firth
and coasting down like Lucifer toward earth
in trumpet spirals, forms that wind and rain
erode from standing stone and souterrain.

Driven off its course, a tousled heron
drags the night behind it like a curtain
and sinks its toes in a hag of sphagnum moss
beside a ringing river. With a toss
and muffled flap, this pilgrim smoothes its plume
and gingerly advances through the gloom.

Eyeing fingerlings beneath a ledge,
the heron whets its gaze on the water's edge.
Its neck, now limp as rope, abruptly bows
and floats a sleeky head above the flow
as in a cobra's hypnotized display.
With a sudden thrust, the bird impales its prey.

Fluid rock, Iona wraps in mist
the island's endless morphogenesis:
addenda, curling up the crust of land,
and corrigenda, subsidence of sand;
addenda, beech and hazel, oak and ash,
by corrigenda burn to smoke and ash.

Gleaned from shafts of sunlight, barley grain
steeps in a tank of Lochan Torr and rain,
the kernels dried in ovens, milled to grist,

oared to mash, the wort drawn off and mixed
with yeast in wooden washbacks, boiled until
its spirit fogs the neck of a copper still.

Heaven blends with Hell. The whisky bears
a nose of salt and peat reek, earth and air.
It warms the belly, blooms, and stimulates
a lucid dream as it evaporates,
pissed away against a public wall
beneath the stars, as summer turns to fall.

In winter, clouds haul water from its source,
the ocean basin, welling up by force
of deep convection through the troposphere
to irrigate the crops and kailyards here,
propelled by the polar jet from trough to trough
across the rippled flats and furrowed crofts.

Kings of the present world, your glories fail,
your frigates founder in a sudden gale:
here lies the *Swan*'s gigantic, bony hull
submerged in silt beneath the Sound of Mull,
a reef for conger eels to colonize,
her ribs dismantled by the rushing tides.

Light rain sifts from clouds in which it's bound
instead of breaking loose to drench the ground:
mammato-cumuli distend like udders,
braiding rills that feed the Forsa's waters.
From smoking haar to affluence to loch,
this long hydraulic cycle never stops.

Masses coalesce as planets, flung
through empty space and spinning round the sun
by force of gravitation while we sleep,
the piles of consciousness embedded deep
in Tertiary basalt, gneiss, and schist.
To such foundations Columkill is fixed.

Not far beneath the surface, all who died
sustain the darkness, cloistered from the sky.
In slow combustion, corpses decompose,
stripped by slugs of feathers, fur, and clothes;
of flags of disposition, yours and mine;
of family, genus, species, kith, and kind.

Of all the dead, not one can read our psalter,
An Cathach, borne through clashing swords—the Battler!
Locked in a cumdach forged from plates of brass,

its leaves have caked and cockled, gone to grass,
and yet its songs still circulate as sound,
escaping spiral form and snapping hound.

Pursuing my own thoughts along a track
across the rocky headland Ardmeanach,
I found a basalt frieze of fossil leaves
and frozen force of trunk in low relief.
This tree outlasted Vikings, Picts, and Jutes,
transformed, but still remembering its roots.

Quarried blocks of Ben More set in stone
the legend of a dead volcanic cone.
Who heard its molten lava hiss and sing,
extruding through the crust to which it clings?
What buzzard climbed a sgurr of ashen air?
What Moses grasped the glyphs eroded there?

Returning day, volcanic spilth of dawn,
instantly overflows the Firth of Lorn:
dies irae, day of humid chill,
a day of knuckles cracking, snow on sill,
a day to counteract a night of love.
From sleep's edge I feel a gentle shove.

Sunlight beams across this beehive cell:
a socket for the skull, a hissing shell
or cochlea, inverted coracle,
it amplifies the laughter of a gull.
This blank stone on which a blanket curled
has heard confession from a savage world.

The ferry sounds its horn, a tuba blown
by Israfel to roust these weary bones.
Illumined limbs untangle, creases fade,
extremities revive. Having strayed
all night, my thoughts return along a strand
of *Helix* snail shells pulverized to sand.

Venus greets the morning sun as Lucifer,
struck against Iona's rocky spur.
Orion slipped the Outer Hebrides
four months ago and left the Pleiades
a fading smudge of fingerprint on steel.
Such tropes revolve like spokes within a wheel.

X-rays pierce a silver Tompion
pocketwatch recovered from the *Swan*:
beneath a calcite crust and hunter case

the sun and moon sit frozen on its face.
Time has stopped. Beleaguered Jacobites
still crouch in caves, arrested in their flights.

"Ye'll Aye Be Welcome Back Again," a reel,
meanders through the Bellachroy Hotel:
hung over or reprised from Friday night,
it emanates from sources out of sight.
On flute and fiddle, fingers leap like deer;
My heart's in the Highlands, my heart is not here.

Zealous dukes and earls have cleared the way
for blackface sheep to trample Torosay
as clachan cedes its place to congregation,
cliff to cloud, and rupture to abrasion.
Flocks disperse from pens; the days unfold
between volcanic heat and glacial cold.

THE ROUGH BOUNDS

I like the sort of track that passes
out of English altogether
as through the Bronze Age bowl
of Glen Moidart, its edges cracked
by forces flooding the drove road
with *wee lochans*. Each excerpts
from sgurrs of Dhomhuill Beag
and Dhomhuill Mór and heaps of Norn
rimmed with mud. The wind whirples
leaf from branch where seven beeches
make a stand. Beyond a white bull
that bears the head of Constantine,
the Coffin Road branches off
to Eilean Fhianain, Finan's Isle
(if road can ever reach an island).
Keep straight, until your tracks
disperse in streams and soggy moss
like final whispered wisps of smouk.
Where you stop, a fald of stane
has folded up its last sheep.

ACKNOWLEDGMENTS

These poems have previously appeared in
Alhambra Poetry Calendar, *The Baffler*,
Colorado Review, *52nd City*, *Free Verse*,
The Hat, *The Nation*, *Notre Dame Review*,
The Paris Review, *Poetry*, *Poetry Daily*,
The Washington Post Book World, and
on poets.org. "The Young Pretender" was
published as a broadside by Woodland Pattern
Book Center in Milwaukee. I am grateful
to the Howard Foundation for support
during the completion of this book.